Who am I?

Rooting a Child's Identity in Christ

by Lucesita Meléndez

Little Light Publishers, LLC

Dedication

This book is dedicated to my loves from youngest to oldest.
My nephews:
Layden Ramón Taylor
William Carlton Taylor IV
Christopher Mark Ondash

My daughter & son-in-law:
Sylvia Santos
&
Joshua Cruz Santos

My son:
Justin Ramón Meléndez

Also:
Mi adorada familia

and
All the precious souls who read this book.

Who am I?

You,
my beloved,
are a
loved child.

John 3:16

Who am I?

You are
a child
of the
Most High God.

Galatians 3:26

Who am I?

And you
are made in
His image.
Genesis 1:27

Who am I?

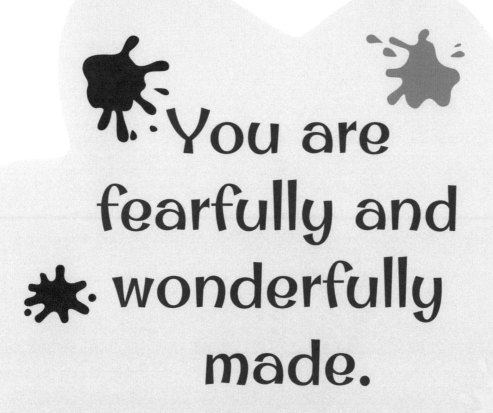

You are
fearfully and

 wonderfully
made.

Psalm 139:13-14

Who am I?

You are a precious pearl.

Matthew 13:45-46

Who am I?

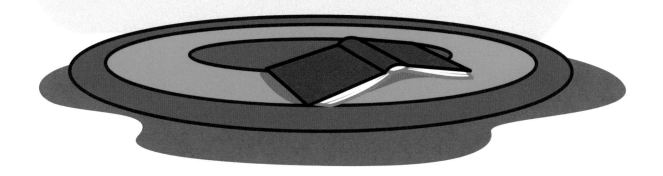

You are chosen.
Ephesians 1:4

Who am I?

You are predestined by God to inheritance.

Romans 8:17

Who am I?

You are blessed when you come in and when you go out.

Deuteronomy 28:6

Who am I?

You are
the head
and not
the tail.
This means
that you
are a leader.
Deuteronomy 28:13

Who am I?

You are above and not beneath.

Deuteronomy 28:13

Who am I?

You are redeemed, rescued, saved. You are free!
Romans 8:2

Who am I?

You are holy, and you are blameless.

Ephesians 1:4

Who am I?

You are
a citizen
of Heaven.
Philippians 3:20

Who am I?

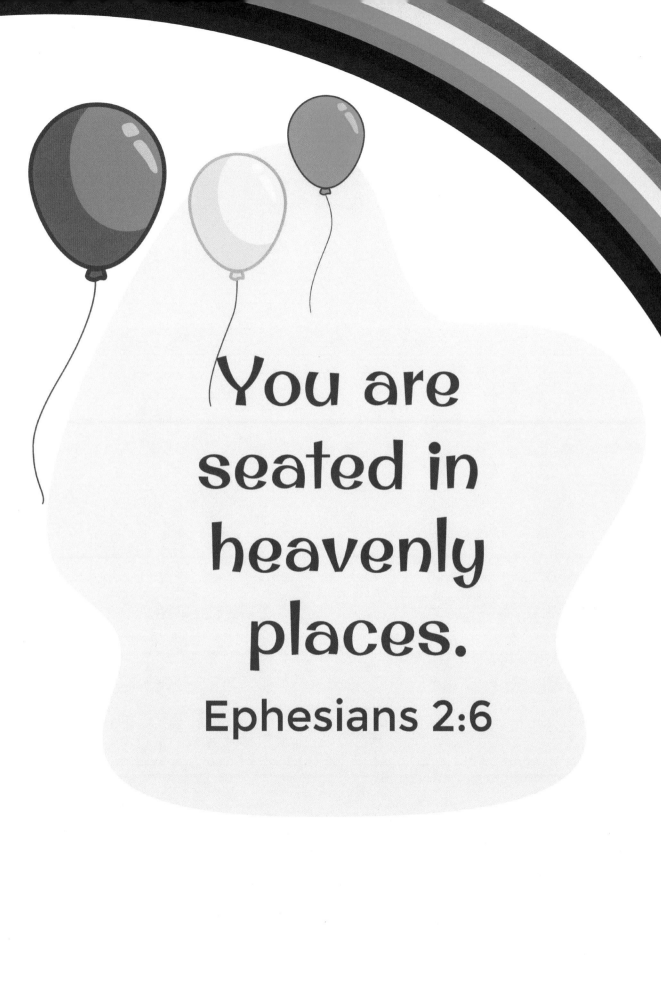

You are seated in heavenly places.

Ephesians 2:6

Who am I?

You are a child of
a King of kings
and Lord of lords.
He is almighty
and powerful.
Revelation 1:5

Who am I?

You are the
child of
the great

I AM WHO I AM.

Exodus 3:1

You are special

You are smart

You are creative

You are capable

You are honest

You are courageous

You are caring

You are adventurous

You are fun

You are kind

You are lovable

You are beautiful inside and out

And now
you say... "AMEN!"
Which means,
"so be it,"
because you
believe it.

To the best parents in the whole wide world: I am very grateful, mom and dad, for all of your love and support. I love you. Thank you.

To the most fabulous sisters in the world: Leticia Darquea and Leida Taylor, I adore you and your hubbies.

Thank you to all of my loves mentioned in the dedication page, just for being you; love you more. Sylvia, you are the best cheerleader any mom can have.

My most humble gratitude is to my illustrator, Cecilia Coto.
Cecilia, you have been a delight to collaborate with. You have been my hands for my vision. Thank you for extraordinary patience along this journey.

I look forward to creating a coloring book with you following the translation of this book into the ten most spoken languages.

Thank you to my English editor, Angela Haywood and Spanish editor, Gabriel Alejandro Chacon Rojas.

Thank you for assisting me in the formatting and publishing process, Adedolapo Ogungbire. You're the best!

Made in the USA
Monee, IL
25 May 2022